8 LOVELY LIES

A HUSBAND'S GUIDE TO WIN HIS WIFE'S HEART

SRINIVASA RAJU UPPALAPATI (LUCKY SRI)

I am deeply grateful to the individuals who have made a profound impact on my life and shaped my journey.

I would like to express my sincere gratitude to **Rear Admiral R. Sreenivas, VSM (Retd)** sir, and madam **Mrs. Harika Sreenivas** for the guidance and support they provided during my formative teenage years. Their wisdom and influence helped me navigate this critical period and make informed choices that aligned with my core values and aspirations.

To my parents, **Mr. and Mrs. Uppalapati Appalaraju and Venkata Lakshmi**, I extend my deepest gratitude for their tireless efforts in shaping me into the person I am today. My mother's guidance has had a profound impact on my life, as she instilled in me a strong foundation of logical thinking, rational decision-making, and a sense of empathy towards others.

I also want to extend my gratitude to my sister, **Mrs. Santhipriya**, and brother-in-law, **Mr. Verma Raju**, for their unwavering care and support.

Additionally, I would like to express my heartfelt thanks to my in-laws, **Mr.** and **Mrs. Subbaraju** and **Varalakshmi**, who have given me their daughter as the precious gift of my life.

Although I may mention her last, she is always at the forefront of my thoughts. I thank my loving wife, **Keerthi**, who has been a constant source of encouragement and support for my passions and shared responsibilities. She was the one who first reviewed my content, and I value her opinion.

I would like to express my heartfelt gratitude to my friends and colleagues, who have consistently provided me with their support, encouragement, and thought-provoking ideas. Their unwavering encouragement has been a valuable source of motivation, and their diverse perspectives have helped me to think critically and approach problems from unique angles."

Finally, I extend my gratitude to my stress busters—my lovely sons, **Kushaal** and **Himesh**—and my nephew **Advith** and Niece **Advika**—for their love and energy. They bring joy and motivation to my life.

Contents

Acknowledgements

I would like to express my deepest gratitude to the countless individuals who shared their personal struggles and stories with me, providing me with a unique opportunity to gain valuable insights and perspectives. The openness and vulnerability demonstrated by the wonderful ladies, gentlemen, and couples who participated in this process have been a source of inspiration and motivation for me. Without their willingness to share their experiences, this book would not have been possible.

Preface

I appreciate your purchase of this book. Before I disclose the reason why I wrote this book, I'd like to share reactions from female acquaintances and co-workers. Here's what they said:

"What sort of title is that?" "We just need truth, not a hoax." "Why did you write a book on this topic without permission?" "It's true that our spouses lie, but we feel happy despite it." "Couldn't you find another topic?" It appears that this book caters primarily to men.

One woman suggested renaming the book to appeal to women, while another joked about the potential protests from women's groups if they were to show up at the author's house.

Why did I have to write this book in the first place? As an observer of human behaviour, marriage has always been a fascinating subject since my childhood. From a legal and social perspective, I believe that marriage is a valuable system that has evolved over the course of human history. However, some spouses and couples now experience psychological suffering for various reasons, such as misunderstandings and a lack of understanding. Many others still lead compromised lives. Even individuals with exceptional personalities often struggle to understand their partners' needs. After counselling numerous couples, I've discovered that certain aspects often go unnoticed yet hold significant importance. I believe that by acknowledging and addressing these often-overlooked points, we can significantly reduce conflicts with our partners and cultivate a more joyful life. To further illustrate this point,

I've taken the perspective of women and explored the issues they face. In doing so, I aim to provide a deeper understanding of women's needs and desires, which can ultimately help men better understand and support their wives.

As I've written this book, I've sought to address the diverse challenges faced by couples from various socioeconomic backgrounds. My upbringing in India, where I was exposed to a range of economic conditions, including middle-class and impoverished families, has provided me with a unique perspective on the complexities of couples from different backgrounds. Through my work across various parts of India, I've had the opportunity to interact with people from diverse walks of life, which has deepened my understanding of the issues faced by couples from different socioeconomic strata. By sharing these insights, I hope to create a relatable and applicable guide for couples in India, from poor to upper-middle-class households, that acknowledges and addresses the distinct challenges they face."

While some examples may be specific to Indian couples, I believe the book will still resonate and provide valuable insights for couples from a range of cultural and economic contexts.

This book will barely take an hour to finish. However, I advise guys to read one chapter every day and reflect on it so that this relationship prescription will produce some fantastic outcomes for all of you.

A Masterpiece of Her Own

ONE

A MASTERPIECE OF HER OWN

The Beauty

In this chapter, I will attempt to explain how a husband should see the beauty in his wife. Please forgive me if anyone doesn't like my attempt. Please forgive me if my description of a woman offends anyone in my attempt to promote reciprocity between a husband and his wife. In my opinion, "Every woman is a beauty to behold, in her own unique way."

Just imagine a situation when you and your wife are getting ready to go to a function together. What will be your answer if she dresses up and asks for your opinion on her attire? What will your response be at that time? Don't stress your mind too much. Here I am giving a few options to recollect your response. As your marriage gets older, the likelihood of your response to your wife will evolve as follows:

'*You look beautiful, darling.*'

"You are looking gorgeous, sweetheart."
'You're looking great."
'You're looking good.'
"Of course you are looking great. Now don't delay further. We are already running late for the function."
"Your dress is good. But... your make up seems a little heavy."
"Baby, you should lose some weight."
"Baby, who is going to check on us? Common, we are getting late."

The right answer to this question is not that simple. Many people might think that saying something like *'You're beautiful'* or *'You're lovely'* would be enough for her. But, in reality, it's not that easy. Your wife wants more than just a simple compliment. She wants you to look at her with love and admiration. She wants to see the admiration you have for her in your eyes. Unfortunately, we, the honest men, never lie with our eyes. We can't show the love in our eyes. Especially to our wives. I have asked many men about their opinions on this matter. They gave me some reasonable justifications from their end. I will try to discuss a few of the logical justifications with my illogical reasoning:

"Brother, the reason I married her is her beauty alone. She always looks gorgeous. But is it necessary to validate her beauty all the time?"

I'm not saying that you should praise your wife all the time. Tell her how she looks to you at that particular moment. Try to say something new instead of the same compliment every time. Take a moment to think about it, and then say it. I can understand that we men are always in a hurry to settle any issue in a faster manner. But don't do this with her. The ten seconds you spend looking at her will surely increase the value of the impression you give her. Try to notice the small changes she made to that particular attire. Dedicate some time to observe her. Appreciate her in your own way.

For example, Just recollect a moment when you wore a new shirt to your office and your colleagues, and your boss complimented you by saying, *"Your dress is nice"* and *"you are looking great today."* Just remember how your day went. You would have worked enthusiastically the whole day. Isn't?. I believe that every time you wear that dress, you will definitely remember those compliments you received from your friends and colleagues. More specifically, the person who first recognized the novelty and uniqueness of your dress that day will not be forgotten so quickly. Also, you can't forget the person who described how you look in that dress in a unique way.

I want you to have such a special place in your wife's heart. Only you should.

"She was beautiful when I married her. But now she is not like that. Why should I lie to her?"

Have you ever been travelling on the road and found a woman in front of you attractive? When the vehicle you are travelling in passes her vehicle, you might have tried to see her effortlessly. Then you might find her so attractive. Sometimes, she may not seem so attractive. It means you liked a particular profile of that lady, right?

"Remember a time when you stood in a queue? And you found a woman standing two people away in front of you who has an attractive rear profile from the bottom of her earlobe to the nape of her neck? Was there ever a time when you waited for her to finish her work and turn back?. Again, there's an equal probability of you liking or not liking her front profile. In the same way, don't you find a single aspect of beauty in your wife?

The reason I am trying to explain all this to you is because I strongly believe that beauty is in the eye of the beholder. I know some of you are going to be angry with me at this point. I will try to make you understand.

After your wife gets ready, capture a photograph of her on your mobile phone. And then take her to a professional photographer and ask him to capture some more beautiful pictures of your wife. Compare both photographs on your own. You will understand the difference. I know what's going through your mind right now. You may give the justification as "The photographer can take better pictures because of the camera with more pixels."

Just think about it once. Imagine how many wonders your eyes with around 500 mega-pixel power can do when a photographer can take a good photo with a 50 mega-pixel camera.

In fact, your wife wants more than just a good photo or a simple compliment. She wants you to look at her with love and admiration in your eyes, just as she looks at herself when she feels beautiful. She may have become a bit chubby due to the aging process, or her hair may have turned gray or thin. She may be busy simultaneously handling her office responsibilities and taking care of your children, but she cannot take care of herself.

The pain of not being able to look attractive to you will haunt her every time she stands in front of the mirror. But even so, she will try innocently every time to see that longing in your eyes again and again, like the way you looked at her before marriage.

That's why, if possible, at least check your wife's beauty like a professional photographer.

"My wife is not blonde at all; however, I hold her in high regard." Why should I lie about her beauty? I won't tell."

Beauty may only mean a glowing complexion and attractive body symmetry in your perception. But take a closer look: from her ankles to her forehead, aren't there any single things you love about your wife? If your answer is yes, try the following:

While talking to your wife affectionately, try to find out if she has received any love proposals from anyone in the past. She may or may not give a proper response to your question. But you will definitely notice a cute smile on her face, which appears and disappears in a split second. yes indeed! She recalled an unknown devotee from her past.

As you gaze into her smile, focus simply on her happiness. Don't compel her to answer your question. If possible, try to see your wife's beauty from that anonymous devotee's point of view. By doing so, you'll not only bring peace to your mind but also foster a deeper connection with your wife. Are you ready to become that anonymous devotee of your wife?

If you are still not satisfied with my suggestion, please try this once.

If you ever get a chance to follow your wife when she's dressed up well and goes for an outing or shopping, just follow her from behind. Make sure she does not notice you doing that. I want you to focus on other people who stare at your wife—it could be anyone, regardless of their gender. Just focus on what they're finding in your wife. I just want you to realize: How come you missed it?

In conclusion, recognizing your wife's beauty is essential for building a strong and healthy relationship. It's not just about physical appearance; it's about acknowledging the unique qualities that make her special. By looking at her with love and admiration in your eyes, taking time to notice the small things that make her beautiful, and showing appreciation for who she is, you can build a deeper connection with your wife and strengthen your bond.

"If you can't, at least try to say, '**You look lovely**".

A Plate of Love, A Dash of Kindness

TWO

A PLATE OF LOVE, A DASH OF KINDNESS

The Food

When your wife asks, "How is it?" you're probably thinking that praising the meal itself is unnecessary, as any flaws are conveniently attributed to the salt or pulses. But, alas, she's genuinely asking about the dinner. So, do you give a candid answer, like "It's a bit salty," and risk facing her displeasure? Or do you opt for a more diplomatic response, such as "Delicious!"? Whatever your choice, it's all part of the art of marital negotiation—a delicate dance that requires tact and diplomacy. This phenomenon is not unique to any one household; rather, it's a common occurrence in many homes. Notably, our responses often follow this pattern, reflecting our efforts to balance honesty with tact and diplomacy. Here are some responses that husbands usually give at the dinner table:

"Wow, this dish is really hitting the spot! The flavours are so well-balanced, and it's just what I needed after a long day."

"You know, honey, this meal is nice, but it's not quite knocking my socks off."

"Sweetheart, I think this dish might be a bit too salty for my taste."

"My dear, I regret to inform you that this meal is not satisfying me at this time."

"You know, babe, this dish has a lot of potential, but it's missing a bit of kick."

"I've attempted to craft responses that mimic a husband's gentle critiques and suggestions, infused with politeness and consideration. However, I must admit that my efforts are likely a far cry from the actual conversations that take place at the dinner table. I'm sure many of you can recall instances where your own dinner table discussions didn't quite live up to the ideal of constructive criticism and warm conversation. If you have any special feedback, please write it in the space above and send it to me. I will print it with your credits in the next edition.

"As a child, I was raised in families where women took the reins in the kitchen, and I've often found myself curious about the dynamics of cooking within my own social circle. I've had conversations with friends who are professional chefs, and I was surprised by their responses when I asked if they cook for their wives. Despite their expertise in the culinary world, they confessed that they prefer to enjoy their mother's or wife's cooking at home. When asked about their own signature dishes, they enthusiastically described their own creations. However, when asked about their favourite dishes prepared by their wives, the answers were more hesitant and took some time to come forth. But when asked about their mothers' cooking, the responses were swift and full of nostalgia: "Oh, that's my favourite dish!"

in order to realize the situation, In the case that your wife is a good cook or not, let us study the many methods and techniques, as well as the approaches that should be taken and those that should not be used, in order to arrive at a conclusion.

If your wife is an exceptional cook,

"If your wife is an exceptional cook, take a moment to reflect on what her favorite dish is. Have you ever sincerely expressed your appreciation for that dish and acknowledged that it's uniquely special because she makes it? When hosting family gatherings or social events, do you proudly showcase the dish she's prepared and publicly praise her culinary skills? Have you ever informed your spouse that you really like a dish best enjoyed when she cooks it and that other people's versions just fall short?

If you haven't already, consider trying these gestures. Find your favorite dish among those she's prepared and associate it with her name. Don't worry about what others might think; your wife will appreciate the recognition and genuine praise. She's unlikely to be concerned with what others think, and this small act of appreciation can have a profound impact on your married life. By showing your gratitude and admiration, you can strengthen your bond and create a more loving and supportive environment."

If your wife cannot cook so deliciously,

Have you ever gone to an expensive restaurant, eaten your dinner, and paid the bill only to discover that it was not worth the meal? Many individuals may have recommended that you try the meals at the hotel. But you didn't like the meal. Will they agree with you that the chef doesn't cook well there?

Some people like to put a little more salt in the dishes they eat. Fewer others. Similarly, our likes and dislikes are very different for every taste, like chili, sour, or nutty. Everyone has the freedom to say, "I don't like this or I only like this," but no one has the right to say that the way you do things is wrong.

What more could you possibly want if your wife is capable of making eatable food? Have you ever disclosed your dietary preferences to her? If you're a good chef, try spending some time in the kitchen teaching your spouse new skills. This will strengthen your bond in addition to assisting her in becoming a better cook. If you are not a good cook, leave her for a few days with your mother and have her prepare meals the way you like. You might also think about getting a personal chef to prepare meals for you at home if your budget permits. In this manner, you can savor a wide range of flavors and cuisines without sacrificing your personal preferences or culinary abilities."

As she learns and grows, your words can have a profound impact on your relationship. Praise and encouragement can strengthen your bond and boost her confidence, while criticism or negative comments can create emotional distance between you and your wife. Remember, every word counts, and it's essential to focus on building each other up rather than tearing each other down."

So, instead of nitpicking the little things, like the amount of sugar in her coffee or tea, try to appreciate the love and effort she puts into making it. Just see if there is the right amount of love and admiration for you in her eyes. When she asks how it is, just say **it's good**, and she'll not ask you again. After all, she knows the truth.

Trust in the Tides of Life

THREE

TRUST IN THE TIDES OF LIFE

Trust

As you walked to the office, you noticed that your shirt pocket was missing a hundred rupees. You immediately called your wife and asked, "*Did you take the money from my pocket?*" She replied, "*I didn't take anything.*" At this point, you had two options: you could believe her and move on to your work, or you could jump to conclusions and accuse her of taking the money. However, it's important to consider the possibility that there could be other explanations for the missing money, such as a mistake in calculation or a genuine need for the money that she forgot to mention. By taking a moment to reflect and consider alternative scenarios, you can avoid misjudging your wife and potentially damaging your relationship.

Here's a further refined version:

Assuming she eventually confessed, saying, '*I took that money. I forgot when you asked, and I took it for household expenses,'* you still have two choices to respond.

Option 1: You could respond by acknowledging her honesty and using the opportunity to teach her about responsible financial management. You might say, *'I appreciate your honesty, but I'm concerned about our finances. Can we work together to find ways to manage our expenses more effectively? Remember, every rupee counts, and it's essential we're both mindful of our spending.'*

Option 2: You could react with anger and criticism, saying, *'This is unacceptable! You're taking money without permission or even remembering it. How can I trust you with our finances?'*

Which approach do you think would lead to a more productive conversation?"

Let's say you are working on a project and your phone rings. When you pick it up, a call from an unidentified number appears. You were shaken by the caller's dire warning, *"Your wife is cheating on you." If you would like further information, I will meet you outside at a specific intersection at 4 p.m. after you leave the office."* He's holding out for your reply.

You're faced with a dilemma. You can either believe the stranger's claims and rush home to confront your wife, or you can take a more level-headed approach.

Option 1: You could choose to react impulsively, cutting the call and making a beeline for home to 'catch your wife in the act.'

Option 2: Alternatively, you could take a step back and respond with skepticism, asking the caller for more information about their claims and demanding to know who they are and why they're making such accusations.

Later that evening, after arriving home, you have the opportunity to confront your wife about the mysterious call. Instead of jumping to conclusions or accusing her of wrongdoing, you choose to approach the situation with empathy and understanding. You explain that someone called you with these allegations, but you believe in your wife's integrity and want to know if she's facing any difficulties that might be causing someone to make such false claims. By doing so, you demonstrate your trust and support for her and create a safe space for her to open up about any challenges she may be facing.

Imagine coming inside your house late at night and noticing a dent in your car that is parked in front of your house. You immediately suspected that your wife was responsible, given that she had taken the car out earlier that day. Your initial response might be to scold her: *'I told you to take the car out carefully, but now it's got a dent. It'll cost 4-5 thousand rupees to fix it.'*

However, this approach is problematic. Instead of jumping to conclusions, you could take a more measured approach and ask your wife what happened. You might say, *'I noticed a dent on the car. Can you tell me what happened?'*

To your surprise, your wife responded calmly, *'It was an accident. I didn't mean to cause any damage.'* She then sat *down*, awaiting your response.

My point is that, as a partner, it's essential to have faith in each other's integrity. Trust is like the water that nourishes your relationship; it's essential for growth and flourishing.

In this situation, instead of accusing your wife or blaming her for the mistake, you could have chosen to respond with understanding and reassurance. You could have said, ***I believe in you. I know that accidents can happen, and I'm glad you're safe.***

By doing so, you would have reinforced your trust in each other and created a safe space for your wife to open up about what happened. This approach not only resolves the issue at hand but also strengthens your relationship over time."

Is it really that hard to show trust when you've been lucky enough to spend a large chunk of your life with someone who has promised to spend the rest of her life with you?

How about you attempt the phrase "*I trust you*"?

A Symphony of Priorities

FOUR

A SYMPHONY OF PRIORITIES

Priority and importance

In many movies and TV shows, we've seen the trope of the leading lady issuing an ultimatum to her husband: "*Do you want me or your [mother/friend/x]?*" While these scenarios are often played for comedic effect, they can be a source of genuine distress for those involved. So, what motivates a woman to give an ultimatum like this? Is it a deep-seated need for validation and reassurance, a desire for autonomy and control in the relationship, or something entirely different?

In reality, husbands often go to great lengths to provide for their families, and they strive to meet the needs of their loved ones. Similarly, many women contribute significantly to their households, whether through domestic work or financial support. Despite these efforts, it's not uncommon for women to feel a deep desire for their husbands to prioritize them in the midst of these responsibilities. This expectation is not always easy to fulfil, as men often juggle multiple demands and obligations. It's likely that your wife shares this sentiment, feeling that her husband's attention and focus are essential to her well-being. However, it's only when she reaches a breaking point, feeling that her husband is not prioritizing her, that she may resort to issuing an ultimatum like the one we discussed earlier.

I'm sure you value your wife deeply, but have you made it clear to her that she's your top priority? Let's explore some ways to demonstrate your appreciation and make her feel valued. Take the time to think about what matters most to her—is it a special piece of jewellery, a favourite accessory, or a thoughtful gesture that shows you're paying attention to her daily needs and desires? When her birthday arrives, take the day off from work and spend quality time with her. Make it a special occasion for both of you, and if that's not possible, plan a fun outing or surprise at another time. Additionally, be attentive to her needs and offer help when she's busy in the kitchen or has time off from work. Show her that you value her by being present in the moment, listening actively, and showing genuine interest in her life. By doing so, you'll not only strengthen your bond but also make her feel seen, heard, and loved.

"I understand that it can be challenging to be with her physically all the time, especially with work trips and social events. It's okay if you can't be physically present, but make an effort to stay in touch by regularly calling and checking in on her. When you return, prioritize dedicating quality time to her. You may have a list of tasks to complete, but make sure she's involved in the process. Come home early in the evening and spend some quality time together. The key is not about what you do for her, but rather showing her that you're willing to go the extra mile for her. Lovingly convey to her that she's always on your mind."

Here's an example of what we could do in the future:

When she asks you what's most valuable in your life, respond with confidence and conviction: *it's her*.

Imagine the scenario where she approaches you while you're spending quality time with your children and asks the question that can make or break your heart: *'Do you like me more or our children?'* In this moment, it's crucial to choose your words wisely.

While it may be tempting to respond with an honest answer, I suggest opting for a comforting lie instead of a heartbreaking truth. A reassuring response can bring her comfort and peace and ultimately strengthen your relationship.

Empowering Her to Shine

FIVE

Empowering Her to Shine

Her Abilities

Have you ever found yourself in a scenario where your wife's enthusiasm and excitement have caught you off guard, leaving you feeling a mix of emotions? It's a typical evening, and your wife's jubilant tone welcomes you home after a long and exhausting day at work. She bursts into the room, her eyes shining with excitement, and says, *"I have some fantastic news to share! Our neighbour Sujata is joining a fashion design course, and she's been encouraging me to do the same. She believes that if I complete the course, I'll have access to excellent job offers and a brighter future."* As you listen to her words, you're met with a whirlwind of emotions: curiosity about the course, scepticism about the job prospects, and perhaps even a hint of annoyance at the sudden interruption. Your mind is racing with questions: Is this a genuine suggestion or just a fleeting whim? Should you take her enthusiasm at face value or probe deeper into the details? Whatever your response may be, it's crucial to remember that this moment presents an opportunity to nurture your relationship, to show your wife that you value her efforts to bring positivity and excitement into your life, and to explore the possibilities that this new development may bring."

However, in this scenario, many men often react with irritation, responding in a way that can be perceived as dismissive or critical. For instance, they might say something like, "*You have no sense of fashion, so why would you want to take a fashion design course?*" or "*Let's focus on Sujata first and see what kind of offers she gets before we decide whether we should do it or not.*" Others might respond with a more neutral tone, such as "*That's a good idea; let's join*" or "*That's a good idea, but how much does the course cost?*" Meanwhile, some men might take a more negative approach, saying something like, "*I don't have the money for it*" or "*Why don't you just ask your father for the money?*" These responses can be hurtful and unconstructive, potentially stifling the wife's enthusiasm and creativity.

Many people who find themselves stuck in a monotonous routine crave a sense of excitement and novelty in their lives. Also, for many stay-at-home mothers and wives, the daily routine of domestic duties can feel suffocating, leading to a deep-seated longing for something more. They yearn for a sense of purpose and fulfilment beyond their daily responsibilities, and they dream of having the freedom to pursue their own interests and passions. As they navigate the challenges of being a stay-at-home parent, they may feel trapped in a cycle of monotony where their days blend together in a haze of laundry, cooking, and childcare. The constant demands of providing for their families may make them feel as though they are losing themselves in the process and that their sense of identity and self-worth are eroding.

In this chapter, I'll look at the common desire for change and progress that many women have as they negotiate this difficult and often isolated profession. By sharing relevant experiences and anecdotes about the trials and achievements of housewives and career-oriented women, I intend to bring comfort, validation, and encouragement to those looking for more out of life. I will also look at how society can better assist and empower women, as well as offer practical advice and solutions for individuals who want to break free from their daily routines and follow their own goals and desires."

I'll never forget the conversation I had with my office senior in Mumbai about 18 years ago. He shared with me that his wife was enrolled in a cake-baking course, and he had invested a significant amount—50,000 rupees—for a one-year program. When I heard the price, I was surprised and asked him, "*Why spend so much money on something that is easily available at a neighbourhood bakery for just 500-1000 rupees?*" He chuckled and explained that his wife had already completed a basic course in cake making, and this advanced course was an opportunity for her to refine her skills and explore her creativity. He recalled that, after just a few days of the basic course, she was thrilled and felt more confident in her abilities. Moreover, her cakes were now impressive, earning praise from their friends and family. My senior's perspective was refreshing—he recognized his wife's talent and was willing to invest in her development rather than simply dismissing her aspirations.

Fast forward to recent years. I had the opportunity to catch up with my senior again, and he shared with me that his wife had actually landed a job at a private company and was earning a handsome salary of 50,000 rupees per month. But what really caught my attention was that she was also earning an additional 50,000 rupees per month as a skilled cake artist.

I feel a sense of admiration for my senior's willingness to recognize and support his wife's talent. He didn't simply dismiss her desire to learn or pursue her passion; instead, he took the time to understand her goals and invested in her development. This story has stayed with me, serving as a reminder of the importance of recognizing and nurturing the talents of those around us, especially the women in our lives.

"I'd like to share a few more personal anecdotes from my own life and those of my friends, which have helped me gain valuable insights into the importance of supporting our wives. Through these experiences, I've come to understand the significance of offering unwavering support and encouragement to our partners, regardless of their aspirations or goals."

I'd like to share a story about a friend who stood by his wife's entrepreneurial spirit. Every year, during the festival season, his wife would order saris from Surat and sell them to their friends and neighbours in Visakhapatnam, Andhrapradesh. I had the opportunity to ask him about the business's performance, and he shared with me that his wife handled every aspect of the operation. She was thrilled to be running her own business, and as far as she was concerned, there were no losses. Any leftover saris were either kept for personal use or sold at a discounted rate to their friends and family.

What struck me most about this couple was their mutual understanding and respect. Recognizing his wife's desire to try something new, he started the business with a modest investment, not expecting significant profits. Instead, he valued the mental satisfaction she derived from pursuing her passion. This story is a testament to the power of supportive relationships and the importance of empowering individuals to pursue their dreams."

"I'd like to share a story about a friend who put his wife's entrepreneurial venture above his own interests. Despite having no passion for the chit fund business, he chose to support her out of loyalty and a desire to avoid hurting her feelings. She had started the business with the neighbourhood women, and he reluctantly joined her in the endeavour.

Unfortunately, the lack of financial management skills led to the venture's downfall. The couple was forced to return the investors' money, leaving them with significant bank loans to repay. What's more, the experience has created tension between them. Despite his initial intention to support his wife, she now blames him for not providing genuine feedback on the proposal. Conversely, he blames her for not considering the financial implications of the venture from the outset. This anecdote serves as a reminder that poor planning and communication can complicate even well-intentioned efforts.

I'd like to share a story about a talented woman who was a high achiever in her studies and worked as a team leader for a software company. Her husband, who worked for the same company, was supportive of her endeavours. However, she grew dissatisfied with her job and decided to pursue a career in government services.

Her husband initially expressed shock at her decision, but he soon started questioning her in an effort to persuade her to remain in her current position. "*What job offers peace and freedom?*" he asked, implying that she should consider the trade-offs of her current role. He also pointed out the intense competition for government jobs and questioned whether she could succeed.

Despite his scepticism, he ultimately gave her his blessing to pursue her dream. Two years later, she landed a government job with a slightly lower salary, but she was thrilled with her success. This story highlights the importance of emotional support and open communication in relationships, even when faced with uncertainty and risk.

What can you apprehend from the four anecdotes I shared above? May be your wife feels like doing something new; She may wish to become a homemaker instead of a career woman; she may plan to start a new business venture; she may want to join a job; or She may simply desire to master a skill as time passes.

That's why I tell you again and again: **Find out the positive aspects of your wife before she jumps into something.Find out what she can do before she gets the idea to do something;** tell her how you can help when she contacts you; even if her plan doesn't seem right to you, first consider the positive aspects of that plan; then explain the negative aspects to her and help her try to find solutions to them. Don't think that she's weak just because she asked for your view and support. She just wants to check whether you stand up by her side, as Jambavan encouraged Hanuman, who was doubtful about his powers.

I believe that individuals, particularly women, should be empowered to pursue their passions and interests without external pressure or expectation. Rather than being forced or encouraged to develop specific skills, women should be free to make choices about their own development and growth. If a woman chooses to pursue a particular skill or talent, she should be able to do so without needing someone else's approval or intervention. On the other hand, if she doesn't feel motivated to engage in a particular activity, it's perfectly acceptable for her to make that decision on her own. It's essential to recognize and respect individual agency and autonomy, allowing people to make choices that align with their values and aspirations. This means that women should be empowered to take charge of their own decisions and actions, unencumbered by external validation or pressure. In the context of the couple's situation, it's crucial to avoid becoming an obstacle to your wife's plans, even if you don't agree with them, as long as they don't harm you financially or socially. By doing so, you can demonstrate respect for her autonomy and support her in making choices that align with her goals and values."

My approach is simple: when your wife presents her idea, acknowledge its value and offer support. You could say something like, *'I think your idea is great. If you're determined to pursue it, I believe you can succeed if you put in some extra planning. If there's anything else I can do to help you, please let me know.'* This approach shows that you value and respect your wife's autonomy while also offering a helping hand when needed."

Whispers in the Dark, Smiles in the Light

SIX

WHISPERS IN THE DARK, SMILES IN THE LIGHT

Romance

Scientists strive to expand human knowledge through experimentation and innovation. While even the most dedicated researchers encounter setbacks and failures, it's crucial to respond constructively and foster a positive team dynamic. For instance, when a scientist has tried numerous times to achieve a goal but has failed, they might say:

"No problem; let's try a different approach tomorrow. Thank you for your consistent support and assistance."

This approach acknowledges the team's efforts, expresses gratitude for their help, and encourages collaboration and creativity. By doing so, the scientist can promote a culture of continuous learning and ultimately achieve their goals.

When a scientist achieves their goal, it's equally important to recognize the contributions of their support staff. A constructive response might be:

"I couldn't have done it without your expertise and dedication. Your hard work was instrumental in making this invention a reality."

In contrast, taking credit for the success without acknowledging the role of the support staff can diminish their contributions and create a culture of individualism. In the end, a scientist's actions determine their behaviour. When faced with failure, they may choose to blame others or take responsibility for their own defeat. When faced with success, they may choose to take credit for themselves or share the credit with others. A committed scientist takes responsibility for their own defeat and dedicates their victory to those who helped them.

It is possible that you are questioning why I am giving a lecture about scientists and the behavior of scientists in order to introduce a significant chapter concerning romance.

I'm sharing this because your bedroom is also like a laboratory. The experiments you conduct in your bedroom will make your married life enjoyable. Here, both of you need to think like scientists. Help each other and keep researching. Regardless of the outcome, you should continue to strive to grow your love. Romance is the spark that ignites a deeper connection between husband and wife, fostering a sense of mutual understanding and respect that permeates every aspect of their relationship. It's the gentle whispers in the dead of night, the tender touch, and the sweet gestures that speak volumes about love and devotion. By prioritizing romance, couples can strengthen their bond, build trust, and create a sense of belonging that is essential to a happy and fulfilling marriage. I'm not prying into your personal affairs, but I believe that romance is the secret sauce that makes life together truly special. Without it, even the most well-adjusted relationships can feel dull and unfulfilling. My aim is to guide you towards a deeper understanding of what romance means to you and your partner and to empower you to cultivate a love life that is vibrant, passionate, and true. By doing so, I hope this book will stand alongside you as you embark on a journey of self-discovery, growth, and happiness."

In a society where openly discussing romance was taboo, husbands and wives have now decided to share their passions with each other occasionally. However, while husbands openly share their desires and fantasies with their wives, some wives struggle to express their desires to their husbands. There are still people who keep their mouths shut out of concern that their spouse won't understand their wishes and desires if they express them. Perhaps due to increased literacy rates or the widespread accessibility of the internet, the situation has improved compared to earlier times, but whether she can openly share her desires with her husband and whether her love is completely free from crime remains a question. As you read this book, you are trying to uncover what she wants. I appreciate that.

When you're enjoying a romantic evening, don't forget to express your gratitude and appreciation to your partner. Let her know what you loved most about her and her actions. **When you try something new to spice up your romantic life, be sure to acknowledge and appreciate her efforts, even if it's just in a whispered moment.** Acknowledge the good intentions, regardless of the outcome. By doing so, you'll show your partner that you value and respect her efforts, and it will strengthen your bond."

The Melody of Unrequited Love

SEVEN

The Melody of Unrequited Love

Love

Have you ever stopped to think about whether you truly express your love to your wife? I'm not asking if you love her, but rather if you take the time to tell her. The responses I've gathered reveal a range of perspectives on this important question. Some husbands say they occasionally express their love, while others argue that it's not necessary to explicitly state their feelings. A few admit that they're too busy or that their wives already know how they feel. Yet others confide that they're hesitant to say "I love you" due to concerns about being seen as sentimental or because they feel their wives no longer need to hear it. But is it really necessary to verbalize our love in order to truly feel it?

Verbalizing love is essential in any romantic relationship. It's not just about saying the words; it's about showing appreciation and affection in a meaningful way. I'll explore the importance of expressing love in various aspects.

Firstly, if you express your love to your wife occasionally, it's great to mix things up and try something new. Instead of relying on the same tired phrases, consider writing a poem or reciting a famous quote from a movie. This can add a touch of romance and creativity to your gestures. For example, you could give your wife a bouquet of flowers on your wedding anniversary or write a heartfelt poem to express your feelings.

Secondly, some people may wonder why they need to say "I love you" to their partner. It is said that every woman was once held on her mother's lap and treated as a princess. and she thinks her husband would shower her with the same amount of love and care. However, males regard women as an equal partner, someone who can help out around the house and provide sound advice when asked. Without a doubt, she is prepared to carry out her duties as a wife. She wants you to treat her like a princess, but she also wants you to treat her like her dad.

Your affection and appreciation will go a long way toward showing how much you care about their growth and improvement.

Thirdly, many couples feel that they don't need to verbalize their love because they already know how each other feels. However, this is similar to going to a temple and not making an offering to God. Just as you acknowledge your devotion to God through prayer and ritual, you should also acknowledge your love for your partner through words and actions.

Many people struggle with verbalizing and expressing their love and affection to their partner, and it's understandable. After all, finding the right words can be daunting. However, expressing love and appreciation is essential for maintaining a healthy and fulfilling relationship. Let's explore some ways to show your love and appreciation to your wife, even if it's difficult.

One option is to surprise your wife with something she likes, whether it's a small gift or a thoughtful gesture. It could be something as simple as her favourite coffee or tea or something more significant, like a gift that shows you've been paying attention to her interests and hobbies. The key is to know what she likes and to make sure that it brings her joy. Remember, it's not just about the gift itself, but about the thought and effort you put into it.

For busy couples who don't have a lot of time to talk, a simple text message or phone call can go a long way. Take a few seconds to express your love and gratitude, even if it's just a quick "I love you." Like making your wife's favorite cup of coffee or tea, there are little things you can do to demonstrate your love and gratitude. You may express your love and gratitude in a big manner through these little acts of kindness.

Some couples may feel that they've been married for so long that saying "I love you" feels like a routine or even silly. However, there's no harm in saying those words, even if it makes your wife laugh. In fact, laughing together can be a great way to strengthen your bond and create happy memories. It's also important to remember that expressing love and appreciation isn't just about the words themselves, but about the thought and effort you put into it.

Finally, when expressing your love and appreciation, consider the importance of sharing your experiences and stories with your children and grandchildren. Sharing your wife's strengths and accomplishments can be a powerful way to show your love and appreciation for her, and it can also help your children understand the importance of relationships and family values. By sharing these stories, you can help your children understand what makes your wife special and why you love her so much.

In conclusion, showing love and appreciation to your partner doesn't have to be difficult or complicated. Whether it's through small gestures, thoughtful gifts, or simple expressions of gratitude, there are many ways to show your love and appreciation for your wife. By taking the time to think about what she likes and what makes her happy, you can show her that you care in a meaningful way.

I'd like to share a heartwarming love story that I know, inspired by real-life events. To maintain their privacy, I've changed the characters' names and kept their identities confidential.

In Rajahmundry, Andhra Pradesh, Mr. Chakravarti, a childhood friend of my father's, lived with his wife Rani. They visited their doctor for a routine check-up, and after reviewing Rani's reports, the doctor noticed that she was physically healthy but mentally unsatisfied. The doctor recommended that she learn something new to improve her overall well-being.

Chakravarti asked Rani what she wanted to learn, and initially, she didn't respond. However, when she finally revealed her desire, everyone was surprised. Rani had always wanted to learn to type, a passion she had put aside after her parents arranged her marriage with Chakravarti when she was still in high school.

If Rani had expressed her desire to learn typing 20 years ago, it would have been more practical and understandable. At that time, there was a high demand for typing skills, and those who acquired this skill had more job opportunities. This was a common aspiration among individuals from various educational backgrounds, from high school graduates to degree holders.

However, in today's society, a middle-aged housewife who wants to try something new often faces criticism and ridicule. If the skill she chooses is not in demand, people may view her as eccentric or even crazy. Unfortunately, this is what happened to Rani. But our Chakravarti uncle did not let criticism deter him. He remained committed to fulfilling his wife's desire, recognizing that his duty was to support her aspirations. As a result, arrangements were made for Rani to enroll in a typing institute and pursue her dream.

The news of Chakravarti Uncle's passing just a few months ago deeply saddened me. He was a remarkable individual who left an indelible mark on those who knew him. Even though he is no longer physically present, his love and legacy continue to live on in his wife's heart.

The respect I have for my uncle Chakravarti has reached a new level. In my opinion, Chakravarti's love and devotion to his wife surpass even that of Shah Jahan, who built the magnificent Taj Mahal in memory of his beloved wife.

That's why I believe it's never too late to express your love and gratitude to your partner. In fact, I would say that time is of the essence. Don't wait until it's too late; tell your wife how much you love and appreciate her, even if it means telling a small white lie: "*I love you.*"

A Safe Net to Fall Back On

EIGHT

A Safe Net to Fall Back On

Dependency

In recent times, I've observed a widespread trend: people are obsessed with the idea of independence and detest the notion of being dependent on others. In my opinion, this extreme emphasis on individualism is a major contributor to the erosion of the marriage system. While the concept of independence may seem appealing, it's just a euphemism for being too proud to rely on others or accept help when needed.

Marriage is a lifelong commitment that requires two people to be intimately connected in all aspects of life—physical, financial, social, and emotional. However, some individuals hold a rigid view of independence, proclaiming that they should not be dependent on their partner. The notion *"I don't need my partner"* is equally misguided, as it neglects the fundamental aspect of marriage: the mutual reliance and support that define the bond between two people. When we say that it doesn't matter if our partner is not physically present, we diminish the significance of marriage and reduce it to a mere phrase.

"I'd like to share two personal anecdotes that illustrate the significance of having a healthy dependence on one's life partner, as it can foster a deeper sense of connection and intimacy.

One afternoon, I had a conversation with my 17-year-old nephew, a passionate food enthusiast, that led to a profound insight. As we teased each other about his cooking skills, I jokingly suggested that he learn how to cook, implying that he wouldn't need to rely on his future wife for every meal. His response was both unexpected and thought-provoking. *"I don't want to learn to cook, Uncle,"* he said, *"because I think it's better to depend on one's life partner. If my wife were to leave me in the event of a disagreement, I wouldn't try to win her back. And if I depend on her for something, I'll do everything in my power to maintain our relationship."* His simplicity and depth of thought struck a chord with me. It was a refreshing reminder that true love and commitment require a willingness to rely on one another and work together through life's challenges."

Similarly, a conversation with a female colleague at work left a lasting impression. When she bought a new car, I asked if she had acquired a driver. She replied, *"I learned how to drive, but I won't. Driving in Hyderabad's chaotic traffic is unbearable. Moreover, I enjoy sitting next to my husband while he drives and chatting with him."* Her response was charming, and it resonated with me.

Have you ever found yourself in the midst of a chaotic workday, juggling multiple tasks and deadlines, and your wife suddenly calls you for help with something that seems insignificant or trivial to you? Is she frequently asking for your assistance with opening a stubborn jar or reaching a high shelf? It's not uncommon for women to ask for help with tasks that would be easily manageable with a little extra effort. However, it's not because she's incapable of doing them herself; rather, she values your input and desires to foster a sense of mutual reliance in your relationship. By helping her in these small ways, you're not only providing practical support but also nurturing your emotional connection. You're demonstrating that you're willing to lend a hand, be present and supportive, and show up for her when she needs it most. By doing so, you're building a stronger bond and reinforcing the importance of teamwork in your partnership.

I want you to be aware of what It's not only about transporting your working wife from point A to point B if she asks you to drop her off at the metro station; you should realize that she's looking for your presence, your companionship, and your attention. Understand that she wants to spend some quality time with you, getting away from the daily grind and spending some peaceful time with you. Instead of trying to analyze her request or explain why she can't just call for a cab, just tell her how much you appreciate her gesture and take pleasure in your time with her. Alternatively, if you are unable to provide it to her, kindly tell her, "Baby, I would like to drop you." However, I must leave for the meeting. Please understand."

Women often yearn for the warm and fuzzy feeling of knowing their husband is missing them, whether it's due to a particular activity or occasion. Similarly, men also experience this sentiment toward their wives. However, I believe that women tend to place a greater emphasis on their partner's feelings of absence and longing. In fact,

many women take pride in saying that their husbands can't live without them, implying that they are so integral to their partner's life that they are unable to imagine a scenario without them.

In today's society, when couples disagree, it's not uncommon for them to resort to hurtful words, saying, *"I don't need you; I can be peaceful without you."* Some may even take a break or try to prove their individuality and capabilities. However, I believe that this approach is ultimately detrimental to one's marital life. While it's true that in today's society, we have the financial freedom to obtain everything we need, regardless of our gender, this independence is not necessarily a reason to abandon our partner and neglect our relationship.

It's important to recognize that a marital relationship is built on mutual support, trust, and dependence. By choosing to prioritize our own individuality and independence over our partner's needs, we may inadvertently dig the grave for our relationship.

What I'm attributing is not that women should be confined to domestic duties or that men should be solely responsible for external tasks. Rather, I believe that both partners should have a basic understanding of essential skills such as cooking, driving, managing household finances, and taking care of family needs. In my opinion, when one partner has stronger expertise in one area, it's not only acceptable but also healthy to rely on each other with love and respect. By doing so, we can foster a sense of mutual support and teamwork in our relationships, which is crucial for building a strong and lasting bond.

While every husband undoubtedly loves his wife deeply, many men often struggle to express their emotions openly.

It's common for husbands to miss their wives when they're apart, but they may not always verbalize their feelings. Instead, they might brush off their wife's concerns by saying "*no problem, I'll manage*," which can be perceived as insensitive and dismissive of their wife's presence—a response that can be hurtful and misunderstood."

In a healthy marital relationship, a sense of mutual indispensability is crucial. I encourage you to nurture this feeling by showing your wife that you cannot imagine life without her and that she plays a vital role in your life.

This time, whenever she has to leave for any reason—whether it's a vacation with friends, a business trip, or a work assignment—take the opportunity to express your feelings. Let her know how much you'll miss her presence, and tell her to come back soon. If you're struggling to be honest, consider saying something as simple as '*I miss you*' to make her feel loved and appreciated."

Thank You

Thank you for reading this book! I hope it has been a valuable resource in helping you understand your partner's needs and navigate challenging situations. If you found it helpful, please consider sharing it with others who may benefit from its insights. You can gift it to a couple who could use a little guidance, or you can recommend it to friends and family.

If you have any ideas for future books or topics you'd like to see covered, please share your thoughts through your review. I'm always looking for feedback and inspiration to help shape my future writing projects. Additionally, if you're facing a specific challenge or concern and think I could offer some guidance, I'd be delighted to help you work through it. Please don't hesitate to reach out to me directly via email, Facebook, or Instagram.

I'm always here to help and appreciate your feedback. Thank you again for reading, and I hope our paths will cross again soon."

* Gmail: luckysriwriter@gmail.com

* Facebook: https://www.facebook.com/Luckysriwriter/

* Instagram: @itsluckysriwriter

9 798895 444313